TEXAS BLIND SALAMANDER FEELINGS

Will Alexander has published numerous books of poetry, including *Refractive Africa: Ballet of the Forgotten* (New Directions, 2021), which was a finalist for the 2022 Pulitzer Prize in Poetry; *Kaleidoscopic Omniscience* (Skylight Press, 2013); *The Sri Lankan Loxodrome* (New Directions, 2009); and *Asia & Haiti* (Sun & Moon Press, 1995). Also known for his essays, plays, and nonfiction, he is the author of *Singing in Magnetic Hoofbeat: Essays, Prose Texts, Interviews, and a Lecture 1991–2007* (Essay Press, 2013), winner of an American Book Award.

Alexander is also the recipient of a California Arts Council Fellowship, a PEN/Oakland Josephine Miles Award, and a Whiting Fellowship, among many others. He has taught at several universities, including Hofstra University, the Jack Kerouac School of Disembodied Poetics, and the University of California, San Diego. He lives in California.

Also by Will Alexander

Vertical Rainbow Climber (Jazz Press, 1987)

The Stratospheric Canticles (Pantograph Press, 1995)

Asia & Haiti (Sun & Moon Press, 1995)

Above the Human Nerve Domain (Pavement Saw Press, 1998)

Exobiology as Goddess (Manifest Press, 2004)

The Sri Lankan Loxodrome (New Directions Publishing, 2009)

Compression & Purity (City Lights, 2011)

The Brimstone Boat (Rêve à Deux, 2012)

Kaleidoscopic Omniscience (Skylight Press, 2012)

Based on the Bush of Ghosts (Staging Ground, 2015)

Spectral Hieroglyphics: A Poetic Troika (Rêve à Deux, 2016)

The Combustion Cycle (Roof Books, 2021)

Refractive Africa (New Directions, 2021)

Divine Blue Light (City Lights, 2022)

Inferential Philosophical Fractals (Second Stutter Press, 2025)

CONTENTS

INTRODUCTION AS PRESENT ASSESSMENT   9

TEXAS BLIND SALAMANDER FEELINGS

THE DUST OF GREEN INFINITY CALLIPERS	13
EROTIC BIBLICAL BEWITCHMENT	14
EMRALDINE LEAP INTO VERTICAL EMPYREANS	15
SOMOLENT EXHUMATION CANTICLE	16
IN THE NETHER DIMENSION	17
DELIRIOUS X-RAY ECLIPSE	18
SUITE AS CONDENSED ARRANGEMENT	19
QUAKING SAURIAN RIVULET	22
PRIMEVAL VISIBILITY	23
TEXAS BLIND SALAMANDER FEELINGS	24
ONEIRIC BIRTH OF THE SUNFLOWER BABY	25
ELLIPTICAL TRANSFERENCE OF PLANES	26
SONG OF OCCULT SOLAR RIDDLES	27
PRIMARY CODA	31
OPALESCENT SHADOW DICTATION	34
INNOMINATE PANORAMA	35
INVISIBLE SAURIAN BALLET	36
LOVE UNDER VOLUPTUOUS AQUARIUM PRESSURE	37
WHITE PHANTASMAL STRETCHINGS	39

PARALLEL DENSITY AS CHARTING: SCRIPTED ANTI-SUMMATION

THE INTERVAL OF DORMANCY	43
BEING AS NEUTRALITY AND DRIFT	45
WITNESS IN TRANSMUTED BAMBARA	47
THE AMERICAN EYE	49
GERMINATION IN POST-OMEGA	51

POETIC METEROLOGY

POETIC METEROLOGY	55
HYPER-SPACIAL ROTATION	56
IMPALPABLE IRRIGATION	57
HYPERSENSITIVE EMANATION	58
FRAGMENT II	59
POSSIBLE PHILOSOPHIC FRAGMENT	60
ON PRE-CELLULAR AUDITION	61
IGNEOUS INVISIBILITY	62

ACKNOWLEDGEMENTS	67

...the blind see with the mind...
— Roberto Matta

...they have put mud over my eyes and I see terribly I see
— Aime Cesaire

© 2025, Will Alexander. All rights reserved; no part of this book may be reproduced by any means without the publisher's permission.

ISBN: 978-1-917617-98-7

The author has asserted their right to be identified as the author of this Work in accordance with the Copyright, Designs and Patents Act 1988

Cover designed by Aaron Kent

Cover image by Will Alexander

Edited and Typeset by Aaron Kent

Broken Sleep Books Ltd
PO BOX 102
Llandysul
SA44 9BG

Texas Blind Salamander Feelings

Will Alexander

Broken Sleep Books

WA

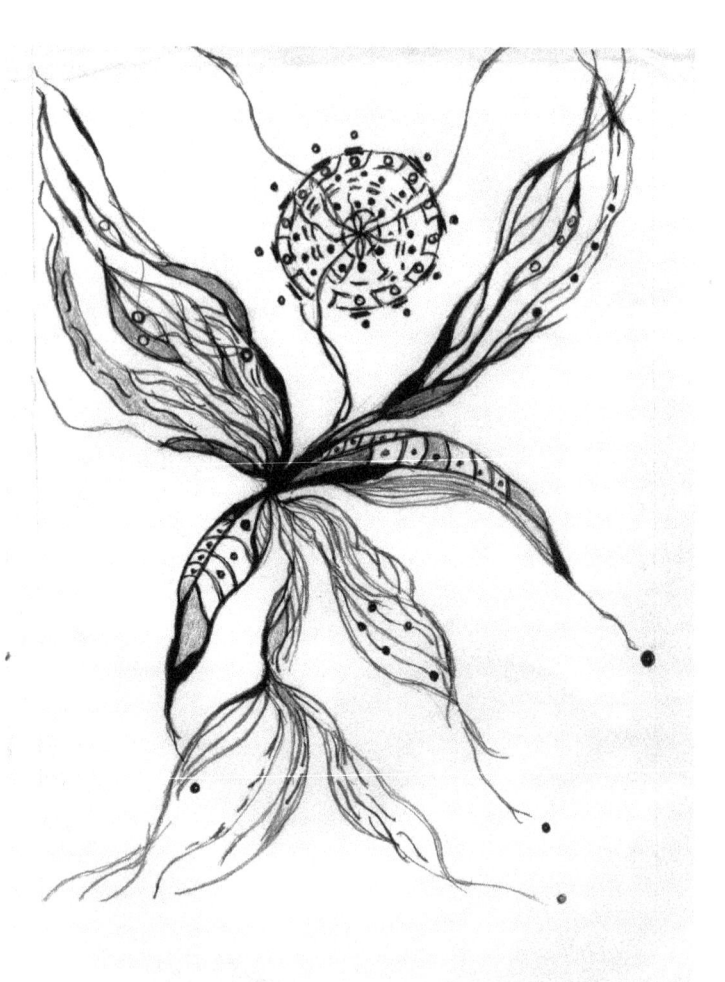

INTRODUCTION AS PRESENT ASSESSMENT

Texas Blind Salamander Feelings was my second book after *Vertical Rainbow Climber* the latter being my first foray into print. Its total content has remained obscured and thought lost for the greater part of forty years. During that period I was empowered by the lingual pulsation that inscribed the work of Bob Kaufman. Aime Cesaire, Octavio Paz, and the lingual/visual grammar of Roberto Matta. Writhing in the wake their collective psychic torrent I began to improvise my own lingual element that had been self-seasoned by my own subliminal tonic inspired by ingesting their essence. Not empowered by principles condoned by rote recall but absorption in the depths of my own imaginative arc as it burgeoned from my own lingual foundation. This document accessed from present distance seemed as one of inevitability. As I go over the original manuscript there were indeed oddities and mixtures that in present seeing having now lost any personal patriotism concerning any personal priority as regards the original scripting. Indeed, the language continues to possess interest for me and persists as susurration not unlike that of unfixed glass capable of forming into fresh shape and formation. In this sense I am reviving Lorca's adage to allow the work time to mature in light of a more mature and lingually balanced maturation. My thanks to the little known Texas Blind Salamander who dwells from birth via blindness in the San Marcos Pool of the Edwards Aquifer native to San Marcos, Hays County Texas. Hearing its curious odyssey immediately propelled me along what I consider a blind automatic expression paralleling what I know of the interesting shapes that blind photographers visually inscribe. Here after protracted sublimation these works have arisen as a new unexpected formation.

The spirit of the opening section as well as throughout the field of the volume more akin to the little known Peruvian abstractionist Fernando de Sysyslo alive with his mysterious colorful magnetic. They emanate via a vocabulary of inner whirlwinds, fractionless novae, never by some distilled pedantic. A field that emanates spontaneous blazing. Not as oblate emblems poised by sterile structural incessance but a structural somnambulism cognitively rendered by a neutral tapestry that condones its own alacrity by lessening. Not in these works the colorless neural register of Robert Motherwell that transpires symbolized by his great work ( )* that I continue to admire. But the praxis of colored works of de Syslyslo seems shadowed by coloured field that continuously roils the imaginal of fields of late Vlamincik not as some strict coherence, but via irregular provenance. The latter power has prevailed implied by the forces of this eyeless Salamander known to the general mind as the Texas Blind Salamander, who symbolizes these works with its ghostly nerve ends invigorated by own inner presence saturate as it is with endemic colour. These works seep from imaginal forces and i as mists that announce themselves as displacement from horizons that announce the innominate spinning of an living realm, not as a province of neutralized carbon but as a charismatic presence that invigorates as liberty living cellular power.

Texas Blind
Salamander Feelings

THE DUST OF GREEN INFINITY CALLIPERS

A voluptuous nightingale of rum
solar osmosis causing moon pressure
spleens of yellowed tar morph to darkened camphor
enjambment embracing me with the dust of green infinity
calipers
your being an arc of ghostly cunning
being scores & scores of manipulated edens
being demonic crosses ingrained in your complication via a
darkened valley of diamonds not unlike an eel that swims through
an arch of sound like a Cassowary magnet
burning like a golden sun under water
being a dietetic aurum
being cobalt samsaras tied to inky eyelid astonishment

EROTIC BIBLICAL BEWITCHMENT

Burn
Nicodemus
burn
in the flashing reversals of decadent Pompeian
metals not unlike fish burning in curious oxide
sewers
rejecting the musical vine of Appolonian ices
with orgasmic eating as perpetual complex
a hedonistic flash of green scorpion innards
erupting as your reversion to pomposity & bile
being deepened barracuda imbibing
seizing monads as pick axe meat
being akin to the older wife seeping out from her
spectrum the absolute Nicodemus
in lewdness
in brush fire complacency
in seaweed miscalculation

Nicodemus bred within the salacious brew of volcanic
droplets stamped with rhetoricians mathematics
with lightning grammatical lightning & blood
being savage enthrallment according to savage first
acts spinning around the shell of a gutted Roman
baker at an anomalous feast of anomalous birds
a demonic conclave of smells
sweltering cottonmouth vines
climbing down the walls of a villa
as an imported Mongolian erotics

EMRALDINE LEAP INTO VERTICAL EMPYREANS

Ejected as solar hurricane flares
not as repetitive coalescence
but as psychic veracity that rises from its own arising
that rises as green feather engulfment
as vertical Indian squalls
of toxins of reddish turpentine veneer
of hidden turpentine veneer
being rotational sonar beyond the dialectical as breaking
point floating beyond the sparking of the beyond
beyond wattage as apparitional spectrum
beyond wattage as cerebral fragmentation
but as incendiary axial mist that ascends into theophanic
havens alive as sonic x-ray aurora

SOMOLENT EXHUMATION CANTICLE

Lonely extended choir of singing
Not unlike insouciant weavings of the spirit gone blind
a sun of its own complicitous rainbow running the gamut of its
own extended fire its tip of grainy dolomite invasions
a spine of rocks vapourized & burning upwards as involuntary
wind being a storehouse of spiders
a tenacious storehouse of bones
being inspired green tin blazing under infested molecules of fire
being zodiac waters mingled with abstrusity
combined with nerve shocks and velvet
being beacons conveyed according to nervous tape worm
oscillations branded by a proviso of wounds
displayed as a seamless variant of itself
that seems to prowl in re-frangible ether

IN THE NETHER DIMENSION

According to blemished salivation
sluggish decimals emerge
more like polished nacre bursts
or splayed nimbus derangements
or a whisp of armour
due to seismic miscalculation

DELIRIOUS X-RAY ECLIPSE

Dreaming in sudden x-ray algaes
that correspond to ringworm antlers
perhaps a smashed analytical chariot
like a twilight as crematorial dimming
a stammering climatic ocher
being an electric flash of nebulae
as a feathered pandemonium chalice
curving with anabolics
being a brightly lit campaneros' fleece
not unlike skeletal pot ash librettos
because time
wandering in the in-illuminable effigies of smouldering
being the Olympian silver phantasmal glassmakers' urine
being a purple sundog as oasis
trembling as wasted evanescence
as audible hieroglyphics
that waken the dead
that somehow smoke out the spirits

SUITE AS CONDENSED ARRANGEMENT

I

Volcanic nuclear spirals
Scattered around the planet
alive as excruciating wind
as flares
become nothingness of the mind
as indecisive transmission
as stunning optical blizzard
as seismic nothingness
become the electric power of seismic ichthuyosaurias'
moraine being an elliptical river of lightning & glass
being teeth as seismic needles protruding
being spasmodic frothing of albino
contusions that crackle as obsidian
reflections

II

The carbonated tundra of the blood
as glowing tidal embers
as Impheyan pheasants
alive as iridescent eruption
as spinning halo lavas wandering the halls of the
dead scouring the realms of hidden interstice
borders being lightning rivers
being Promethean volcano ethics
being obsidian ringlets
alive as elusive philosophical meridians

III

The salamander being blind
as disfigured lumbar region
being sundial mirror as reflective fuse
having in this regard the hematology of
camels understanding in its cycles
how does the universe transpire?
what are the keys to the mystery?

QUAKING SAURIAN RIVULET

Pale trout
flooded indigo spider
never condensed as analytical
chariot as quaking saurian rivulet
in the wind of its quaking brush fire
canals with its ouroboric stellar
antimonies
with its non-existent retinal penetration
being an optics of greenish bone
reverses

perhaps an eclipsed transparency
opaline registrations as spells
of bodiless evolutionary vistas
being a fumarole of transparency
being juggled infinity
astroidal in origin
like the amber of a lions' brew
condensed as underground saurian arrangement

being abyss as solemn stumbling
akin to central thickets of the Sun
alive as fiery waterfall waterfall saliva

as perfect muscular suspension
it blazes as a spectacular uranium
tourniquet as obsessional rhodopsin ballet

PRIMEVAL VISIBILITY

Being movement according to shattered shellfish legs
peering into its own blinded regions
as hypothermic spell
as silent decibel of a blown open star
as oneiric optical lens
cutting through the empyrean's depths
ingesting the burning domain of eternity

TEXAS BLIND SALAMANDER FEELINGS

Its sight
as operant head hunter's prisms
as disrupted turpentine sparks
being strange electrical notation
being incremental fire notation
as creeping cellular incantation
being an implied boar's snout burning
that rises to a strange polarity of emanation
to a kind of photon slumber
to a circuitous radiation historicity
not unlike the molten intarsias of primitive axons as
whisper as a strange optical spelling
akin to quivering ocelot's totemics
because its attempted sight being a forgery of shapes
like the Irminger current flowing within the deep barbarian steam
of a ruby as if it saw a random circumference of worms
a parasitic forgery of shapes
as loops of spinning electrons as silver

ONEIRIC BIRTH OF THE SUNFLOWER BABY

Gusts from roiling ghost stream waters
from intrauterine scalpels
being flooded rainbow hookings
in a torrent of tropical sunbeam blood
this being fire from the sunbeam baby
with stellar aroma
with the boiling nature of its cerulean
defense with its non-existent skeletal
absorption

this being its demise as cathartic
with its physical liquor as salt
its scavengers' metaphysics
being a narcotic anvil burning with contusions

its blood a ghostly yet distributed vermilion
akin to crystalline eternities
floating in the wake of scratchy scorpion tattoos

ELLIPTICAL TRANSFERENCE OF PLANES

Under this plutonium turpentine shifting
there exists analogy with burning Syrian spasms
akin to immaculate village blazing
like elusive rising when it rises as elusive hydrogen wings
above scratchy helium doors
above the herniated fauna of riveted indigo spiders
astrally active like weightless osmium lizards
slipping through the planes
above flaming ocular territory
transmuting its tensions into diaphanous lilies
of higher crepuscular waves above the terse flask of saturnian
stamens above geologic osmosis osmosis
freed of tangled fire scattered along a mythical sunbeam ballast as
heightened evanescence
above bio-physics as exclusive diorama
above neo-crepuscular forums
into sundial radiance of hot white arachnid orientation

SONG OF OCCULT SOLAR RIDDLES

SUN
cut off at the nerves
become a blinded blood cycle visage
erupting from its bottoms
a smoking hemlock transparance

SUN
scorched
revelational
serpent smears
amorphously split by a galaxy of comets
whirring in the cosmic dust of hummingbird negation

SUN
Eating Dahomey colored serpent crystals
a cataract of flesh colored gentian abstractions
& it's flames
Herculean
vertically leaking into victorious skeletal futures

SUN
lightning suit hissing
& the cosmogonic recognition of heated gum erratums
being a sore confused
in the daily muscle of sharded elephant fiber
like a giraffe of flashing serpent stamina
the cryptic flood of embryonic flotillas
inside the bloody astronomical fish salt of the heavens

SUN

as serpent alive with otherworldly radium teeth
stretching its embers into immortal claw mark gases
being a circuitous root as icy Hottetot magma
being python crippling humming a heavenly paradox of axe
riddled blenchings

SUN

as green alchemical volition within powerful potassium arteries
empowered as afterworldly asteroid kinetics
having a powerful saw in its poison

SUN

a throne where indigenous chiefs fission as glow as paradoxical vibration
as clavicle of eel feathers
never akin to modern incessant as deuterium
but as apparitions spawned from vaporous ophidian chronicles
springing from a summit of greenish lunar copper as a perfect mirror of serums

SUN

extended from a molecule of ravens' fire
being ancient blood erupting circuitously spinning within
internal intestinal revelation

SUN

the ozostomia of the earth exploded
its flaws superseded
according to thermal expenditure
expanded the galaxy that is The Sombrero isolation

SUN
& I think of Garga & his burning pole that is Indian astronomy his
magic Indian Orions
his re-ascendant stars as telepathic electrical nodes as
explorational invisibility
Garga
as perspicacious verticality
as perpetual metrics swarming his eye
with a sea of scarlet serpent wings
being a somber vocal geranium

SUN
fluidic & sprawling
as repetitious ultramarine eternity
alive as spectacular evolution
alive in scorching micro-emptiness
& I say sun eater
meditational scorpion oneirics
molten jade bell eternities

SUN
as phosphorescent spiral
as shadow oil
as clairaudient bloodstream

SUN
as powerful eclipse jewel
as arisen sanguinary omega as fertile living soil
in the Marsians
in the Ophiogenes
in the clan of the Senegambia

casting as its spell alchemical python dice
invisibly worn like an alchemical Armilausa
as protective impersonation
an ambiguous cultural aurora

SUN
kinetic as is the silver that swirls as nightmare obsidian not unlike
a purplish Appaloosa kindled in the waves of the Syrian Orontes
its waves black
its seasonal activity as edenic brutality alive as telepathic erratum
as Euphratean tailspin irrigation
possessing the scorching telepathy of exile lavas

PRIMARY CODA

Because the sun burns
as deepened dragon fang as fire
looming in an icy monastery of peril
emerging from empty downpour obscurarion

from its purely hexagonal gulfs
it becomes a livid avalanche of canticles
pouring from anomalous turbity
from Mayan frost driven calculations
from slivers extracted from vectors
not unlike altered rains from hostile pituitary acids
because solar force exists
there is felt an imperishable honour falling from imperishable rain
hands

being a whirlwind from crystal lava trees
encircled by clouds of Persian butterfly pyrotechnics
not unlike dialogical enunciation

so perhaps the mind quivers much like the mystery of porcelain
lion harassment
with its meteoritic equators
as spewing dialectic
as incandescent solar brooks

it implies its dragon numerics warring
as to whether the soul should be split
as to whether a juncture should be inscripted
throughout the risky jubilation of darkness

a jubilation of fleeting rattlesnake compendia
being blank neutrino winds
as sun blurred infinities
flowing cosmic narcolepsy vents
like a marine contraction
swirling as instantaneous photon blizzards

the Sun being phantasmal symbology
whirring like a dermatoid ribbon
or freshly flecked crystal
being ocher rubies or
Saturnian quatrains of agricultural Tsunamis
not a web of avernal wheat
as if demonic by way Lupercalian humanoid vibration as
if its volcano had erupted into sonorous endurance into
sundial alteration
as fire splays itself without blinking
as would alien cortical stems
for instance the release of newts
springing from solar Andromedan cascades

so as a prior sun
as puzzled utterance river
that splays from the depths greenish iceberg squirming as
if lit by phosphorous squirmings
coloured by communal Indian integument

I fertile of fertile lion rhymatics
boiling termite flowers
velvet solitary riddles

as the sky expands
& becomes weightless
as do astral flames from an African green mamba

this becomes as organic solar voice
as mesmeric anis rivulet
being a splayed star boiling in the branches

OPALESCENT SHADOW DICTATION

All the sumptuous optical monstrosities
erupting from Spartan barnacle infernos
cloaking themselves
in an aura of hailstone mazes
in an aura of blood-fish tornadoes
being in the end an opalescent sorcery crackling like spells
paraphrased via parakeets biology
yellowed
via a paramorphic chain of luminescent flashing
being microscopic phosphines transmuted to flares in greenish
northern lands

INNOMINATE PANORAMA

Being a rush of myth & vapour
there exists a poetic flare from seeming jackal's blazes
appearing on the seeming technical plane as froth omniscient
nebular refraction

here
the scarlet base exists of bluish jaguars' ink
such as Swans inside the ash of seeming polar initiation
not unlike the dialectic of water having the power of fire as
vertiginous emanation

being an imaginary meadow of ferocious bleating
akin to sound from smoking sanguinary flowers
evolving into higher & higher hackias of crystal
into elliptical meridians
far beyond protoplasmic complication

one then sees then a realm of lighted Impyean pheasants
flying in circles around a lighted Unicorn's palace
that electrically proliferates as ozonal spell
as osmotic snow
being flakes of weightless jonquil
transcending darkened dragon fang auroras

INVISIBLE SAURIAN BALLET

A throat of quaking obsidian rivulets being blinded Salamander optics
that issue as wind from its sight less brush fire canals
from the depths of his sightless Ouroboric Stellar antimonies
into the outward darkness of non-existent retinal spinning

an optics of greenish aerial reverses being a heraldic dust storm
as eclipse being highly veiled opaline registration

being of higher interior transparency springing from higher
rain demon bonnets being a sigil condoned as porcelain Lion harassment

this saurian
christened as surgical invisibility
as sudden hydrogen glass coloured via the tone of an amber loins'
mane while drifting entering the central thickets of the Sun
thus
heating its fiery waterfall saliva
being spiders spun into curious astral magma
thus
its alter egos suspension
going out like a flare
its twisted shape
none other than obsession
none other than obsessional rhodopsin ballet

LOVE UNDER VOLUPTUOUS AQUARIUM PRESSURE

A Voluptuous apparition of rum
being seepage from dark ozonal moons being simultaneously of ice & black camphor
pulling me into blue-black gematrias of feeling
into a whirling constellation of whirling iridium needles
producing oils & whirling burlap phantoms being your scorching red integument spinning as combustion
as telepathic alignment
as cloudy nightmare blinking
being a state of cloudy carnivores incisors via di-limited irradiation
burning into the void of the way I see blackness

not unlike a streak of mange on your throat or an eruption of lies twisting themselves into sigils
attempting to embrace me with bullets or glycerine
being dust from eruptive saliva
being shadows cast from your lips possessing scores & scores of manipulated Edens
being demonic crosses which ignite from decimation
akin to eels that cross a valley of diamonds

& these diamonds crossing being occulted suns drowning at dawn
being perfect lake's of carbon
being salted glass as charisma
as I enunciate myself as aural yield
hearing your body
as shape

as witness

as cobalt samsara

humming as phastasmatos via glints

WHITE PHANTASMAL STRETCHINGS

This potency, this glow of origins, this flash of fiery charismatic, being hair storm meteor-itic, emerging from deeper worm trigger darkness, being epileptic triangulation of ethers casting spells, amidst Annubic gamma ray mandibles, projected through ghostly arcane scarlet of the emptied skeletal body, not unlike coronas, not unlike oracular forms spun from velvet hurricane registration, like saffron blowing from primal soothsayer windows, being kindled gold veins of the invisible, being the starry graphite of elliptical lotus concentration, being a great Islamic pilot light of Sufistic casidas, they the optic mouth of Angelic geysers, they being mirrors of diamond and jade, they being conveyance of rapid crystalline reflection, as spontaneous Byzantine whirring, as miraculous power of conjunctive rainbow edicts casting spells from cerulean jasper, with all vertical motion gone blank, emitted across the sky as white phantasmal stretchings

Parallel Density as Charting:
Scripted Anti-Summation

THE INTERVAL OF DORMANCY

Think of spores being aloft de-intensified across distance, the ambiguity, the haze, the obscure and contradictory momentum, bled of context, of contorted memorial definition, their motion takes on ceaseless-ness as combined and rarefied disjunction, this is the character, the arcane reflex, of liminal anti-edict, slipping beyond a me of mirrors, where the optical can no longer judge its @8]er as plagiarized de-cohesion, nor crowned deleterious kinetic magnetized by rays of dis-invigorating gravity, what persists as seeming lawlessness, lost-lessness propelled by anaemia, the spore, as fatalistic condensation, kinetic with rare and sub-architectural sonics, it's pre-structured debility, sans hierarchical encasement, sans recrual or illumination via a well-mapped valley, this is not celebration as in discovery by fire, of valuable ore as granite, not pantomime by commitment, or in-delicate fragmentation, nor garish human statement by supercilious invieglement, never confirmed territorial advantage, or seeming codes that plummet to seeming merciless a-rigour, within the random sweep of exploded sedentary Chrystal, this being distance beyond the seeming bloods' advantage, as to bucolic, as to sclerosis condemned to law or pattern, the latter ceases to co-here yet eroded at the core by supercessional ambiguity, for the spore, Aboriginal lightness, symbolic acuteness by raven, wafting, ceasing to know its own engulfment, as to common oneiro-critical establishment there persists non-awakened blankness, not unlike a formless Allamanda mural, by which higher dispersal, supra-coherence no longer adumbrates or multiplies, by its suddenness that arrays and devolves, never extreme dissolution, yet, it's mercury, it's whole advantage via the void, yet non-limited via the void, never as proof by delimited right example, but as directionless drift across the organic febricity of nothingness, its untraceable atoms never condoned by what is known as the dypyptich, of culminate divisibility, it's invisibility invades as drift, as primeval tapestry of heightened molding waters, not to appear as seasoned reflex by calligraphy or subsequent glossary as purgation as faculty by parameter, its inevitable existence via its depth as sporulation being undesgnated root, as non-retentive noetics, not unlike blankness of a spotted crate or an American sora, or a linguistic sporangium, being gyrational refinement, outside the non-contaminant, or diseased theocracies, there is the drifting, the leakage, the prime amnesia of existence, where persistence accrues, not as diagonal theocracy, or reaction by involuntary nerve length, or unclaimed migrational burin, beyond exploded scales, beyond ceaseless regularity of cold, with moons aleatoric with comets, therefore, Dormancy is not a stanchion or alien prognosis by ritual, not one territorial measure is valid, it's pre-invaded gulfs non-sufficient, there exists only the critical irregularity of living, alive with blinding baronial gulfs, with exploded lustrums of torrential claustrophobia, wafting beyond imaginary harbors, beyond steppes of phantasmata, never implying those industrial rooms that suffocate pre-disposed to necrosis...

BEING AS NEUTRALITY AND DRIFT
To Sulubika beyond your unblemished haunting style of alien sonic forces

Being drift, beyond the essence of vermiculite wailing dimensions, being sound elliptical with ambiguity, these neutralized washings of seeming dearth, poised on the plane of seeming inaccessible boundary, by notes as motion, of certainty as integer, no longer at war with themselves, as cause and counter-cause, this being life beyond cause and counter-cause, beyond random loss and adjustment, beyond avowed centimeter heightening, this become drift as uncertain manger, as miraculous kinetics, that spawns its on phantoms, without human grief as uranium cunning, spawned by wails of potential, not as precise and calculable edict as cipher, without power that explores itself, yet reacts not unlike a meandering cipher, being silence as to the diametrical voice, as a pilgrim of interior mathematics, not as secondary distance or biology as stasis, or drowned wires in vapour, thus seethes obliquely concerning task summoned from surreptitious harvest, not in a savage or personal sense, but as an inveigled Heron given up to free existence mesmerically breathing beyond its nuclear aorta, that shadows itself with a form of neutral intensity, within incorruptible projection, thus interminable spells of electrical probing leaving analysis ones kinetic as analysis by abyss, by wafting, staring through regions of autonomous divinity, being source as evolution, as non-declamatory current, a sunless mono-deminson, capable of any Sun, of any angled lightning procedure, being true gradational centigrade, being unfixed molten in tune with higher Stellar indifference, thus, true figment as it exists in transition via riverine galactic, being outside the sway of reason as optic, of course, the outer world with its paltry perturbation, its monstrous back and forth assaults not unlike hellish guano, quickly salting its aura as a darkened hydrogen domain, thus, it's blistered barricades blistered by disappearance, foretold human anatomy anomalous burgeoning with self-copy, like an unforseen tornado or moth copy giving signals concerning suns and their explosive entrails, thus, the zodiacal remains sans its glossary of bastions being light via its non-existent nuclear quilt, not being precise and impeccable as guidance, but as generating glow that eclipses fixation, being symbolic wheat as trans-dimensional glistening, being intra-cellular guidance as rain, not as cracking by compounded crystal.

WITNESS IN TRANSMUTED BAMBARA

A nascent being playing with a bread doll the way moons roar over diaphanous gorges, never as transfixed inclusion, where one seems snared by ocular moray amies, so as addendum, as ocular Moray addendum I confront my intangible odyssey, my haunted Bambara expertise, freshly wakened to the circumstance, to the strange jugular treatise of living, not yet a sage, only a minimal witness to my dazzling embryo of dust, not having gained the rightful measuring answers, not having secured the tribal scars that give me tribal status, as to the why and of tested and retested conundrums, as to the why and wherefore of ones perishing, with ones eyes clouded over with arisen nigredos, with sums that fail to conquer confusion, with clarifications that stammer in ones newly arisen cortical context, why was one born in this oracular context, within its gullible breach?, why have human geologies been suspended?, why have wayward expenditures of God been ignored?, his axial ferocity?, his duplicity ?, because when mountains fall there exists human neurons stinging, breech points scalding, like colossal migrations on fire with treasonous ignition, then one listens to ones breathing, limbs quaking against a wretched shift in the poles, their strain pushing towards geological solemnity, mentally scaled across a savage elixir, thoughts not unlike divinity, wayward, hierarchical with blenchings of dazed sierras, condensed in purple and vertigo remonstrance, in ironic risks, in torrential hypothermia, owing these assaults of weather to the Saxons, progenitors of this general demise now suffered, with criminal ozone leakage, with assumptive behavioural ruinations, by clauses that delimit, by strictures that poison the causeways, by we inherit analogy, who spin in runic mirrors, who spin in verbal parsec, in the last shrill hours of reason, because insight tells one that the tropics have been detached, that the final fauna of Asia has been hidden by Buddhists within a mantra of magic, realia tells us that the last seven centuries have devolved into psycho-human blinding, with instincts fallen, systemic mania newly arisen, as for dread, as for renewal divine majestic, the logos opts for the former, the latter having been subjected into corrosive invasion, as for the Christos, as for the God of the fallen Saxon Sun, there exists a heart, an acid, a baleful declension, that traces its symbol to a stony creed, that remains a disruptive boralis"

THE AMERICAN EYE

To overcome the circumstantial menace that vetted has vetted menacing Saxons, their icy and mechanical abduction of Aboriginal spawning grounds, their deficiencies, their essential vacuums, their mechanical heinousness, of their sordid and lugubrious land capture, underscored by swirling omens, now deepened mangroves for catastrophe, for the bound and particular inversion sighted in daily devouring statistics, their wasteful diurnal mechanics, simply, the plain fatigue of evil, with its in-illuminal ethic of stunted watchtower cobras, always counting by electricity survey the fact of its nervous toxins by strike, its cunning praxis by strike, it's bewildering ornament by cunning, it's seeming replica by law, in its demasted and saturnine procedure, there is glare of the falsely concocted, the glare that is falsely wondrous, the intoxicated, the measured and reduced alembic, portrayed within the tenor that remains one of a perpetrator, tainted, alive as emboldened recessive, with cryptic delay in its genes, now fallen into snare by blunder, not unlike the eye of an old Roman jailer, with a clinical discharge of pus, injured, spun by a ray of psychic red carbon, of deadly brush fire in-melodia, bringing the old accrual of hidden trauma, no longer the ballistical suite of doves' blood masking its errors, therefore, summoned to the heat of collective cortical fires, let us say, that peasants have extracted from infernos a delirious grandiloquence, a felicitous caravan of jade, that dishonors rapacious personas, such as the boiling fount seemingly renewed by collective Herons, they, having the power to issue the pragmatic, attempting to gain in its prisms the lifeless power of exploded arcana, say, America with its ruthless veneer, with it's sums cherished by Invicta, it's lucid momentary burins carving into rice adders digesting tourmaline portions, developed by obscure logic Ian's, summoned by rancid meteor, by dismal practical thirst, by the antiseptic scale of dismal practical thirst, that seems to pursue honourable regularity, being thought within the void of dispatchable glints, therefore, to sum scales on the ground of perfected laterality, always scattering mazes, beyond integers that petrified, thereby rendering schematics, the latter, production of bone and spittle, in reaction, one must deploy old energies beyond simple treasonous expenditure, possessing energy that inveigles all monarchs in the mind, all the cinders that calcified as neatly placed splinters grown to gargantuan magnetic, so the phase that is the popular persona, that builds by umbilical advancement, so each duplicitous inscription that ensnares by duplicitous paradigm, lures exterior stasis by crucifix, whose stasis blocks rays, whose singular incitement seals off the Sun, with its ingress as geo-political devolvement, it's saturnic counting itself by sullen dystopia, by deranged myopia, with it's labored epileptic, oppugnant, ferociously oppungnant with blinding ...

GERMINATION IN POST-OMEGA
Why not embody impermanence...
Huinening
  — Sixth Patriarch in Zen . Buddhism

To persist as flask, as nocturnal monoron, completely unadorned by distant sets of judgment, a wayward nautical elixir, probing simultaneous zones refracted and spun beyond gregarious and spilled topologies and beacons, beyond each known inference of carved delusional facts and grammes, for instance, blankness as it exists beyond the ampersand, non symbolic of the turbulence engendered in profound and absolute extinction, but as an emptied and invincible volition without the terminology of transition, or propulsion without bleak electrum in its forays, there exists neutral thirst of momentum subsumed above the balanced ray of opposition, the lightness solar coast with its minerals in diffusion with its itinerant prosthesis by compound within its dormant alchemical emission, this is the internal carrier, the swimmer across Suns as alien myomycetes as orbits throughout various Stellar condensation, say, the shape of miraculous Hellebores tuned by a-demonstrative pulsation, by realms that link carbon with scarred and torrential magnets of heat, with raw creative transference, the spore by its nature amidst the yellowed heart of suspension, amidst caliginous soporific engulfment, amidst hidden and toppled pyres in various proto degrees across prolific colouration of neutrality, of various guiles of potentia, above the apex of signals, the spore consumed by ironic, by vibrational wavering being fecund storms between dimensions in which a cloud of selenium or cobalt, or the unprecedented tungsten elemental, as in the phase of protracted nuclear electrics as with scandium, or beryllium, so that the sum of its distances from any fixed or general point is non-specific, is the factor where geometry absconds its merciless eloquence with photometry of mirrors as shattered elongation, of disembodied emulsion, being rudiment, taking on sulfurous candescence as liberating haze,conflicts ceasing to evolve from any populous matter, from any seeded fixation, as if, all dimensional conflicts were broken and left inchoate beyond in-fixed eternity, as anti-mesmerization, as to one single bearing, or tendency that occludes adventitious graces, that flow via inordinate meta-kinetic, alive with beatific occultation, as to the anti-sired, as to hollowed nursing evanescence, not Hesperian or auroral, the latter being the flight of the spore, symbolized as trans-galactic simoom, beyond the dice of craft, beyond motion as counted fate, there persists convergence, not only as extinguished hermeneutics, but as the selfless void of Ravines ...

Poetic Meterology

POETIC METEROLOGY

Not as ostentatious solar current
or personal clarity by wisdom
or systemic clarity by peril
this being solar current never according to directional stagnation
as prevalent stationary scale rendezvousing with its own singularity
as if its solar state had de-occurred
blinded by its own solar diagnosis
not by circuitous spectral dust
or by blinding gramme
as f solar regulation as a form of scent that explodes seeding its
own turbulence by animated deftness by kinetic silver lightning
not as kinetic by carbon infested sharing as form
or as glimpse the gains description by supernal cavity
as mathematical malfunction

HYPER-SPACIAL ROTATION

Scripted according to the capacity of compound isolation an evolutionary whirling of levels that translate to cellular blizzards that magically as hyper-states, as impalpable caverns that rise and transmute consciousness. For the individual these psychic cellular states cast transparent wattage that authors inscrutable singularity as pattern alchemically contending with friction itself. This being a level where one can never be scripted as toneless cartographical blankness but where communication plies itself with riverine telepathy overarching fragmentation. One becomes attuned to borderless grammar, at one with pouring psychic waves, sans ideology from compound quotidian scale that then persist as crystal-like, charged with an interior kinetic that issues from rotating figures in the mind. They, being none other than imminence, as stunning peripheral figures casting implausible wavelengths from shadow. There then exists a living realm of emission from less direct planes that authors itself as optical aurality, so as to hear via anterior modest of that erupt as spectacular hybridity.

IMPALPABLE IRRIGATION

As ignition worker forced to interpolate spells Ir remain counter to sodium as exterior proof. I constantly embrangle my seeming power to exist by winding auric diamonds as seeming capturable entities. Thus language rivets as photonic blazes, as impalpable irrigation. The cells then tend to function as operatic sundials, as substrates that cohere as magical largesse. For instance, numeric blazes condemned to states that issue as mirrorless fractions, as beauteous equations. Perhaps as curious solar tornadoes, say, electro-magnetic projections across trans Neptunian fields.

HYPERSENSITIVE EMANATION

Not broad or garrulous inaccuracies but refined exploratory drift evolved as proto-micro diagnosis. At this plane of sensitivity a dispatch of nerves explore themselves via vigorous angles that subsist as intermingled wave lengths. For instance, a blue correlation of mirrors that function as impalpable devices empowered by analytical recitation of fighters spawned inside of opaque dimensions having nothing in common with utilitarian belief, yet something that exists beyond registered finding that registered in terms of palpable of palpable result. Because the dark remains stored by means of caliginous registration it never beams as a three-dimensional saturate that summons itself as an unmoving noun. I am not speaking in terms of grammatical punctuation or the brutality of stationary conquest pattern, but as electrical residue as hyper magnetic insight.

FRAGMENT II

As for cosmic bio-legality
it fails
by inference
as higher persistence
not according to numeric dawns
not according to fragment as skill
as for arc as embellished dragon
it burns as interiority
precarious myths occur
attempting to broker their magnetic
not solely as wonder
or frictionless maze
not as harried cornucopia or spell
this being conjoined sensation
as palpable root akin to impalpable. confusion

POSSIBLE PHILOSOPHIC FRAGMENT

When language continues to cater and impalpably Calculus, it remains stilled, to warped by catering to a populate kinetically brazen with deficit. The scale populated by the living dead as it continues to ignite protracted regression. As partial continents of ice remains active with dissolution it trespasses inactive response with further, more active decimation.

ON PRE-CELLULAR AUDITION

Not as meandering kinetic
not as stationary nexus
not as a planetary water plantation perhaps as raw metrical
hydrogen by oblique dissonance
b raw territorial posture
by crystallized territorial charting
as ostentatious solar current
or systemic via wisdom
or omnidirectional stagnation
as prevalent stationary scale
revolving by prior state as de-occurrence. as shaken spectral haven
as blank combustive cinder
by diagnosis as script
that endemically rises via primodial
regulation
by kinetic imprinting
perhaps scripted tentacles
as malleable silver cascade being outer. grams within fraction-
ated... human presence
that registers its own drifting

IGNEOUS INVISIBILITY

To live for the mystical leap, for divine alchemical combination one must cross this worldly ring with buzzing imperturbable utopian aristocracy, able to live within the basic understanding that time has been exploded and the dragon of doubt been de-nuded along with plutonium geysers spurting rattlesnake combining as verbally engendered strychnine magic, that literally turns igneous realizing from their astral geysers ascendant perpendicular morphine plumes, thus one speaks of a cosmic revolutionary who engenders by this act plasticity whereby immortality leaps like a flying gunner from the habitual proclivity that is death, and the earth becomes one quick silver paradise of haunting, and not and not unlike a scribe of paradise and without flexion calculation as instantaneous existence, not unlike incalculable hibiscus blizzards, the revolutionary within this ethereal degree, of excess as power seems snared in luminous monsoon rain, that transmutes to natural solar psychology that progressively links the temporal with the a-temporal, as one ringing global diphthong ladder, thus the voice of consciousness becomes an emblem, becomes a discontinuous Eddie that suddenly fuses as inward novacane phantoms, not unlike whispers from totality alive in the hieroglyphic chambers of the blood, not only contagion between being and non-being, but between generations beyond human conception, symbolic of primeval patterns and other space-time connective whirling as unknown galactic symbology, that organically signals organically signals the unimaginable that empowers incessant magical vapours of the spiritual Sun, with its infinite bird space that looms and transmutes, the damaged nerves of reflex, of human habitation as it opts for vainglorious presentation, as it opts for false imperial grandeur, with the soul blanked out by the body, the spirit seemingly summed by religious erasure, and what prevails are planetary provincial kingdoms summed by religious erasure, and each part of their spectrum, hoards a kinetic ideal, provincial kingdoms, and each part of their kingdom hoards a spectral ideal, thus a private human state of privatized self capture, and the bloated state of privatized self-capture, drafting the soul with interior spotting as static, therefore procuring an agreement to keep the apocalypse brewing, exploring form between primordial thrust and the form it engenders, so that death seemingly vanishes as brinkmanship flailing, or simply a cross between both, never as simple or believable logistic, there persists absorption of mind in the metrics of peril, of clotted skeletal cinders, for scouring the very habit and movement of destiny, yet there is a qualitative kinetic, of genuine regalia into seeming disappearance, not unlike a horned wildebeest swallowed by a serpent, the former warped by twisted microbes as lesions, resulting in opaque geriatric compounds, being a maze as a form of psychic muscular arthritic, of myopic leukemia, yet there persists existential challenge to surcease, not only plaguing biological considerations within metaphysical isolation, yet, operant beyond cellular hallucination, as the empyrean invades the principle mind with Stellar spores, transmuting to lightning-like power being intergalactic dawn beyond de-limited human dialectic, at one with instinctive threading, fused with the arrow of eternity, being aural yield as supra conscious possibility, thus heliocentric immortality in the cells, as looping architectural certitude, perhaps ghost as ascendant hawk that ascends through the icy altimeter of the Trojan planets, sans power as verbal centigrade, sans poisonous nitrogen kilometers, these being specifics of optically strangled ghosts, within the disappearance of silvered sun traces, not as a dispersal of remnants, but into transparent consciousness, as magical torrent seeping into primordial crevasses, etching subdued flare by osmosis, not as in dense micro-biological wooden blazings, not unlike having the power of a transmuted Heron as it rises into amorphic infinity ...

LAY OUT YOUR UNREST

www.ingramcontent.com/pod-product-compliance
Lightning Source LLC
LaVergne TN
LVHW040424240825
819359LV00039B/682